The

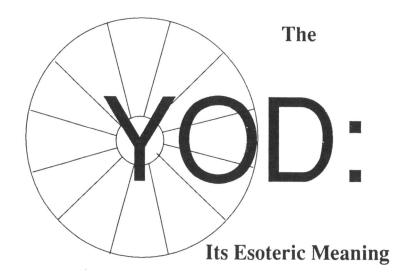

YOD:

Its Esoteric Meaning

JOAN KELLOGG

AFA

First Printing 1989
Second Printing 1992
ISBN Number: 0-86690-369-0
Library of Congress Number: 89-85997

Cover Design: Lynda Kay Fullerton

Published by:
American Federation of Astrologers, Inc.
P.O. Box 22040, 6535 South Rural Road
Tempe, Arizona 85285-2040

Printed in the United States of America

FOR
THE BOOK GROUP

for their constant support
and radiant energies

TABLE OF CONTENTS

PREFACE

It was at the 1984 Chicago Convention of the American Federation of Astrologers that I first presented my theory of the esoteric meaning of the yod. The presentation was very well received and since that time I have continued to apply the principles of this theory to my practice which has resulted in consistent clinical confirmation of this theory.

The preliminary evidence would seem to suggest that the theory that was first proposed at the convention, and is now presented in this book, is workable and most helpful to the professional astrological and psychological practitioner as well as the amateur astrologer.

FOREWORD

The purpose of this book is really to clarify much of the mystery that surrounds the yod. It is not intended as an astrological primer so a certain amount of knowledge is assumed in the style of writing.

The book was also written so that the practicing astrologer can apply basic information of a specific case and situation. Just as each individual is unique so, too, is each astrological chart. The ideas presented here are intended to serve as a base upon which the delineation may be enlarged and expanded.

The astrological community is an endless source of creativity and ingenuity. It is hoped that this book will serve as a catalyst for those who have not yet tackled the yod but have the ability to synthesize and integrate data and who will apply the principles set forth in this book in ways yet unknown. It is the opportunity to provide this information for astrologers that is the real joy in writing this book.

My theory for the yod did not develop out of any serious study of the yod - on the contrary. While reading Esoteric Astrology by Alice Bailey, it suddenly occurred to me that all of the theories about the yod were incorrect. So much esoteric information handed down through history has been written to be intentionally obscure and misleading. In the esoteric astrological context, we have the same problem because so much of our astrological literature has been written from a mundane perspective.

It is hoped that this book will help to open the door for a greater understanding for those astrologers and students who, like myself, have studied the yod but found incomplete answers and results.

THE YOD:

ITS ESOTERIC MEANING

CHAPTER I

THE DEFINITION OF THE YOD

The yod, sometimes referred to as the double quincunx, is considered to be a major configuration if it appears in a chart. It consists of two 150-degree aspects referred to as quincunx or inconjunct aspects. Together these two aspects form a "V" shape configuration in the chart.

The inconjunct aspects share a common planet or angle, which is designated as the "Foot" of the yod. The other portion of the yod is two planets or a planet and an angle separated by a 60-degree or sextile aspect at the top of the "V" formation. Each one of these planets or angles at the top of the yod I have designated as a "Hand" of the yod.

Between the two "Hands" of the yod is a midpoint of the two planets or planet and angle. This I refer to as the "Activating Point" of the yod. This is the most important area, esoterically, in the yod. The midpoint and the "Foot" form an axis, a polarity in the chart, which constitutes the "Axis of Awareness" within the configuration itself.

In the illustration (Figure 1) the reader will note that the two "Hands" of the yod have been joined together. This results in a new "Y" shape configuration.

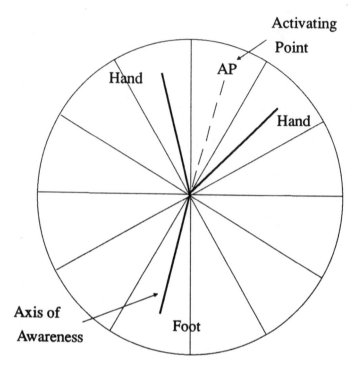

Figure 1.

The yod can consist of a configuration between natal planets, cardinal angles (1st, 4th, 7th and 10th), planets and angles as well as temporary yods created by major transiting planets such as Jupiter, Saturn, Neptune and Pluto or progressed inner or outer planets. The transiting or progressed effect would, of course, depend a great deal upon the individual's readiness and preparation to respond to the very spiritual and refined nature of the yod aspect to have it properly activated.

The matter of angular orb is important for the yod because of its very powerful and important nature. It would appear that a few liberties have been taken with traditional orb rules in order to "make" the yod work, but experience has indicated that a wider orb in the inconjunct angles, up to 10 degrees, may be allowed for the yod, especially with the stronger planets. The yod energies are subtle and the individual can determine whether the yod has been activated by the presence or absence of its energies in their life, not necessarily by the precision of a mundane measurement.

The particular planets and angles that comprise the yod, of course, give that yod its particular qualities. With all of the research advances in astrology, I am very receptive to the possibilities that other celestial aspects such as Uranian planets, asteroids, etc., can also be used. Uranian planets are clearly powerful, as subtle as the yod itself, but I have done little research as to their effectiveness within the yod in comparison to the traditional planets. The same is true for the asteroids.

There are thousands of asteroids, many of which when taken within the context of other aspects, may be of significance. However, a single asteroid taken by itself at one of the points of the yod is too weak to be considered, especially with such a wide orb as can be allowed for a yod when activated. However, a single asteroid in conjunction with a set of midpoints, a solstice point or Arabian point, etc., will add flavor to the overall aspect and should be evaluated.

The exception to this can be found with the four major asteroids: Ceres, Pallas, Juno and Vesta. These seem to be particularly strong and are often seen when the emerging feminine energies within the individual are struggling to surface and be utilized. Therefore, I would suggest that any of the four major asteroids be used as a point in the yod as these are especially significant when they simultaneously conjunct a planet or angle.

I have found that a series of midpoints in very close proximity can be read as a point of the yod, although delineation can be a bit tricky here, it is nonetheless representing a type of energy which the individual reports as present. In the case of a midpoint stellium, look for the most commonly occurring planet in the midpoint stellium and use that as a focal indicator of that stellium's energy.

The Activating Point is derived by interpolating the midpoint between the sextile of the Hands of the yod. This midpoint and the Foot form the Axis of Awareness. If planets natally, by transit or progression, fall at any of these points in the yod, they strongly emphasize the meaning of these points and the overall power of the yod itself.

The Activating Point is important from another perspective as well. In physics there is a term referred to as resultant forces. This is the idea of the midpoints. In other words, somewhere between two energies there lies a mutual field of energies, morphogenic fields where the two energies merge. In the center of this field is the area of strongest attraction. How well these two aspects blend is critical to the functioning of the yod. It is at this point that the yod is potentially at its strongest or weakest.

In the configuration of the yod, the Activating Point symbolically is the "Head" or that position in the yodal figure where a head would be drawn to complete the drawing of the Foot and two Hands. This is an important analogy because awareness and enlightenment occurs in our mind, not our feet. It is between the Head and the Foot that the Axis of Awareness is formed. Along this axis their mutual energies can interchange and blend until such time as they are clarified. The Activating Point is a synthesis of energies, special and particular energies that are unique for an individual's earthly yet spiritual contribution.

The Activating Point is a perfect representation of the Uranian midpoint system and Uranian texts can be helpful in synthesizing and delineating the energies of the yod. In the Uranian system the yod is a natural planetary picture, and it is for this reason that I feel that the Uranian planets should be seriously considered for study and research. As I understand the Uranian system, these planets are the result of calculations of planetary movements resulting from the influence of planets not yet discovered. Very esoteric stuff indeed.

The reader is referred specifically to read two very good books on this subject: *Rules for Planetary Pictures* by Ludwig Rudolph (Witte-Verlag) and *Midpoint Synastry Simplified* by Karen Ober Savalan. Both should be invaluable tools in yodal analysis.

Astrologers who utilize asteroids might find Emma Belle Donath's books, *Asteroids in Midpoints* and *Asteroids in Synastry* very helpful.

5

CHAPTER II

WHAT IS THE YOD?

It was during my astrological practice that I discovered the true significance of the yod. Many authors refer to the yod as the "finger of God" aspect, designating it as an important and often spiritual aspect in the chart. The idea being that the finger of God was an indicator of special talents or a mission to fulfill. Emphasis was typically placed on the Foot of the yod indicating that it represented an area of special importance in the life of the individual. This depended upon the area of the chart that the foot occupied. Just what this significance was was never known or revealed and there was not further information given to the reader.

There is no doubt that the yod is indeed an important energy force in the chart, but my experience has challenged some of the previous theories on the yod and its interpretation in the chart. From an esoteric viewpoint this is not surprising because most, if not all, esoteric delineation involves a hidden energy to an aspect that is not revealed until such time as the soul is ready to handle the energies involved. Granted this is a bit nebulous an explanation, but in actuality there is no better or more accurate an answer.

My clinical experience has revealed several important concepts about the yod. First, on an esoteric level, the yod can dilute, even contradict, some otherwise very strong mundane natal indicators in the chart. Second, its positive energy and power is thwarted until active efforts are made to correct its mundane effects. Thirdly, the yod represents the open door to higher spiritual service and knowledge when its mystery is unlocked. It contains the message and the direction of the life's mission, often hinted at intuitively but seldom understood by the individual.

The yod configuration represents a specific mystery, containing within its geometry a key to a spiritual or karmic lesson that must be learned before its power can be released. *The mundane karmic lesson is represented by the Foot and the esoteric mission by the Activating Point.*

Previous writers have emphasized the Foot as the powerful indicating point of the yod a bit my experience has indicated that it is at the Activating Point of the yod that its energies are esoterically strongest, not the Foot. Our earthly tendency is to choose the line of least resistance, that which is easiest and least difficult, what is commonly referred to as our feet of clay. That makes the Foot of the yod very powerful in a mundane sense. We can and DO get stuck here. Spiritual seekers will know that it is not the easy road that develops character and strength for service, but it is the road of responsibility and discipline that prepares one for spiritual growth.

The power of the yod, the Activating Point, lies dormant until its power is stimulated. We have to remember that most of us, although we aspire to be spiritually attuned, are still very much connected to our personalities, our earthly selves. Were this not true, we would quite literally not have had the need to incarnate. The planets in the

7

chart can only vibrate at the frequency of our personality and soul development. Yodal planets, those planets and angles that constitute the yodal configuration, are no different, and will vibrate at their true, usually lower, frequency unless developed. The yod reflects karmic influences as do other planets in the chart. Often one or more of the yodal planets or angles may begin to vibrate at a higher frequency than the others creating in some instances an unstable and unbalanced condition in the individual.

I have found the presence of instability in many individuals with a yod. They seem to be in various states of lifelong transition causing them sporadic inconvenience and disruption in their personal lives. When the Axis of Awareness is activated and the energy begins to flow from the Foot to the Activating Point, the yodal energies begin to synthesize, creating an harmonious blending of unique energies. The "Y" shape then symbolizes an esoteric tuning fork. Much like what occurs in our inner spiritual centers, the chakras, the vibration of the yod, and indeed of the chart, is heightened and rebalanced resulting in a different interpretation and utilization of cosmic energies.

Typically, what causes this initial stimulation of the Axis of Awareness is the internal timing of the individual's soul. Some factor, event, condition or karmic cycle has changed or occurred to indicate that something has ended or is in preparation to begin. If aspected planets are at all connected with the yodal configuration and its planets or angles, then the Axis of Awareness is stimulated and both the Foot and the Activating Point are stimulated to create a polarity effect, a sort of rod of initiation. This energy is typically intuited long before the actual timing occurs. It is as if the individual had an awareness of an internal blueprint that could only be developed at a certain time or under certain conditions. This is the "mission" aspect attributed to the yod. The individual is almost always aware of this unique area of his of her being where he or she may experience a portion of his or her life as a disequilibrium within an otherwise balanced existence. The yod indicates the iconoclastic individual, the one who doesn't, indeed esoterically, shouldn't or couldn't, fit in. This is the strident individualist in the specific area that the yod energies represent. These energies can only be harnessed from within the individual. This, too, is intuitively felt, but most likely not accepted or truly understood.

In this sense the yod is doubly powerful because an individual can and does become stuck in an issue or condition that the Foot of the yod represents. This is, indeed, the lesson, to release the negative energies at the Foot. The strong individualistic nature of the person will emphasize the negative energies of the yod and create quite a difficult and problematical personality, and if nothing else, a completely underutilized one. *These individuals know that they are unique but do not always know how to express this uniqueness.*

This is an important psychological and emotional marker in the chart because although the yod is always an aspect of potential, one must be reminded that until personality blockages, imbalances and issues, especially those represented by the Foot, are worked out, no true spiritual work can begin. As in anything spiritual and esoteric, no efforts are wasted, but can only be considered preparatory until such time as one is an appropriate channel for their true work.

The individual with the yod has an unusually difficult spiritual road because it is only through the lessons represented through the Axis of Awareness that the individual can truly serve. Their lives are directed to that purpose and that is why they often seem to have such a narrow focus, either at the Foot or the Activating Point. This is a life of spiritual discipline whether they accept it or not. The discipline must come in those areas indicated by the Axis of Awareness.

It is an unfortunate situation that so much of the recent and popular literature about spiritual development and philosophy gives the distinct impression that spiritual growth can be like a quick fix, something to the effect that once you have the idea you've got it. Nothing could be farther from the truth. Discovering the idea is only the beginning, then one must begin to live and apply those newly found principles. This may take many lifetimes. It is true that as a planet our spiritual awareness is increasing as we approach the Age of Aquarius, but what that really means is that very quickly the universe is having to separate the wheat from the chaff, those active participants from the inactive sideliners. An individual with a yod feels the need to participate, and feels this potential but is too often repelled by the idea, usually because it will involve the relinquishment of some inappropriate but comfortable perceptions.

Others will see the potential in the individual with the yod, but it will remain a confusion until such time as the individual is willing or free to continue his or her spiritual path. It is almost a test of wills between the personality and the soul, as if the individual is in a state of complete denial or unawareness about this subject. Indeed most likely it will be until the Activating Point is stimulated. For the

10

astrological practitioner a yod is very difficult to deal with in this manner because the individual who is being counseled will feel quite unfulfilled and yet unwilling or unable to let go of the Foot's influence and rise to the activating point's potential. Like the Jupiter/Saturn polarity, and the lunar north and south node effects, the Foot, our Saturnian taskmaster, will insist upon complete payment and discipline before the Jupiterian rights, privileges and benefits are released.

In many cases, the individual with the yod will appear to be lost, wasting very gifted potentials because of a need to stay grounded or stuck in his or her pattern. It is not necessarily a happy or beneficial pattern but it may be a safe and unchallenging one. If this is the case, then, psychological therapy is recommended to gain personal insight into the source and reason for the blockage. It is only through inner awareness and insight that this is resolved. After all, our earthly problems are just that and need to be solved and resolved in an appropriate earthly manner. Esoteric work is of another dimension but does require physical energy as a conduit. So the idea of working on psychological problems should be regarded as one of many correct and balanced approaches toward solutions of both a mundane and esoteric origin. In other words, an attitude is an attitude and just because it is karmic does not excuse it.

One of the significant double binds that I have experienced with individuals with the yod is that they often know that they are out of balance and would seek therapy if they could find a suitable therapist. Unfortunately, the majority of therapists are clinically trained, and this is excellent for those requiring clinical assistance such as medication. However, this type of training is ineffective with the individual who has problems that are mundane but whose source and solution are distinctly esoteric. These special esoteric therapists are few and far between but should be sought after nonetheless for it is within this context that effective help can and must be found to unlock the yodal energies.

A key to karmic weaknesses can be found in the yod. The qualities, energies and rulerships of the planets and angles of the yod, especially the Foot, will influence and indicate the areas of imbalance in the individual. For instance, the Moon at the Foot of the yod will indicate maternal, mothering and nurturing issues that need to be resolved and learned. These qualities may be more or less subtle or obvious, but they will be present.

There is another way to understand the yodal energies. The Axis of Awareness is like an opposition effect between the third and ninth houses. The third house represents what is referred to as the lower mind, our earthly, mundane, daily mind with its varying levels of education, training and functioning. The lower mind refers to the attitudes, opinions and perspective of the individual. It reflects the learned lessons and patterns of communication of early life. Mercury ruled mundanely, it indicates an easy distractability and represents the lesson of discretion, discernment and discipline. The ninth house astrologically represents the more mature mind, our philosophical nature, higher emotional aspirations, religious and educational interests and pursuits. It also represents the highest ideal we can aspire to in our earthly life. Jupiter ruled mundanely, it represents the ability to expand one's world through study, aspiration and travel. This can be on many levels, the highest of which is the soul level.

While presenting this material at the AFA convention, one of the participants remarked how the yod resembled a bow and the Axis of Awareness an arrow ready to be released. I thought this a particularly marvelous illustration of the thesis of the yod's operational mechanism, latent power and energy. The symbol of the bow and arrow is important, too, because Jupiter, the ruler of the ninth house, is the ruler of Sagittarius, symbolized by the Centaur, half man, half beast, who holds a bow and arrow. The yod esoterically is truly a ninth house, Jupiterian influence. When operating positively it reaches for the heavens, but when operating negatively the arrow remains quite literally in the quiver, muddled down with unproductive thoughts and activities.

The third house/ninth house concept is an important one in understanding the significance of the yod in an individual's chart. The third house portion, or Foot, represents the personality attitudes that may hinder, restrict or limit the individual. These inappropriate ideas limit the individual's soul growth and must be eliminated and released before any real progress begins. True growth can only occur when the mind is focussed, actively aspiring and working towards a purposeful goal. This happens by primarily working on personality issues. The third house/ninth house polarity, this Axis of Awareness, represents the classic battle between our lower nature, our personality and our higher nature, our soul. The personality is here to work on symbolic third house issues, those ideas that the personality, not the soul, holds dear. They are in their essence ideas that in some manner isolate the individual from the rest of humanity. The personality, as

13

represented by the yodal Foot, can struggle to remain unenlightened or release the self-imposed bonds and grow toward its natural goal, the symbolic ninth house, its soul.

The Axis of Awareness represents the weakest areas in the personality. The Foot will dramatically indicate the specific area of needed attention. It is almost as if this is the single most important area of an individual's life that must be addressed in this incarnation and through this personality experience much excellent progress can be made, once the energies are rightly understood and acted upon. In some way, these higher energies will serve to reunify the individual with the greater group.

A yod is one of several quick reference tools within the chart to indicate karmic issues and complications. Specific issues may be difficult to pinpoint but with careful questioning of the individual during a thorough interview the individual's karmic purpose can be clearly detailed and delineated. Personal experience and attitude are the two most obvious karmic indicators and the yod will intensify and exaggerate these personality aspects in essence making the job of the astrologer easier and more quickly focussed.

An important point to remember about counseling an individual with a yod is that a yod is by definition a spiritual aspect and most usually also a karmic one. When we begin to discuss karma with someone we need to reinforce a few of the key ideas about karma. The most important concept about karma is that it is not always punitive. It may indicate a certain weakness in thought or attitude. It may also indicate a lack of completion in some portion of the soul's growth. It may also indicate an opportunity to learn and become more universal through a common or uncommon experience.

In other words, karma is not always a past life debt with a present life payback. Karma means obligation, first to oneself to grow, not to remain static. Opportunities for growth often come in converse ways. This is the idea behind the yod and this is most often why the essence of our karma remains unrecognized and its correction, in whatever manner, resisted. This is human nature. The importance of the yod indicates both where we need to learn and grow and where we resist. This is indeed a helpful dynamic for even the most advanced soul.

It is our karma because we need to learn something, develop an attitude or perspective about something that we don't already have. If it were so easy for us to adapt this new attitude the lesson would not have to be in the guise of karma. It would be easy. What is karma to one person is duck soup to another.

The idea of a yod almost has the inference that we are so resistant to an idea or perspective that we are in need of a cosmic push to get the new idea integrated. We do not need a cosmic two-by-four for the small things, just the big things like our soul and its development. We are our own jailers in a way and we are also our own liberators. It is our attitude that either imprisons or frees us. *The presence of a yodal configuration in a chart indicates that there is a very important need to have a particular idea or set of ideas integrated and thoroughly learned through experience in order that the soul may progress.* It may be that there has been some malingering in past lives or just a necessity to speed up the soul's growth and progress or the growth and progress of a larger group through the focussed effort of the individual in this lifetime. Judging the point is always futile and inappropriate, but finding a suitable way out is correct and meaningful and this is the job of the esoteric astrologer.

The yod is truly a karmic aspect and my experience has shown that the Foot is a tremendously powerful aspect in the chart. Often indicating the area of our greatest resistance, all other aspects withstanding, this resistance is not always conscious or intentional. Clinical experience has indicated that the resistance is due to unpleasant earthly experiences, most probably karma set those experiences in motion to reinforce the meaning of and importance of the lesson, but they serve to set up the entire lesson plan and serve to indicate where the personality has a "foothold" and needs to be released.

CHAPTER III

SYNTHESIZING THE YOD IN THE CHART

The initial delineation of the yod can be done in a simple, methodical manner, utilizing standard astrological principles. It is only later, when interpreting the fine nuances of the yod that real interpretive skill is required. Since this is not intended to be a basic astrological text, I would refer the read to any number of excellent texts on basic delineation, specifically, March and McEver's *Only Way to Learn Astrology* series as well as Bloch and George's *Astrology for Yourself*. These are well written books with excellent information. Michael Meyer's *A Handbook for the Humanistic Astrologer* should also be most helpful in delineating some of the finer points and for grasping the philosophy of esoteric concepts.

To begin the delineation of the yod, the points of the yod need to be determined. The planets and angles, Ascendant, Midheaven, Descendant and Imum Coeli, are the most important and easiest factors to distinguish in determining a yodal configuration in the chart. When a yod is determined, pencil in on the chart the "Y" shape configuration. Highlight the planets and angles and note the orbs. Next, interpolate (find the midpoint) between the two planets in sextile aspect, the Hands of the yod. This is the Activating Point (AP) of the yod. When the Activating Point is located, draw a line from the Foot to the Activating Point and label this the "Axis of Aware-

17

ness." Note the house where the Foot and Activating Point are located.

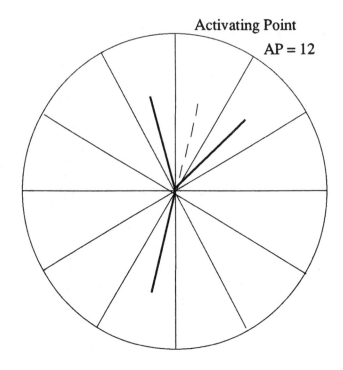

Figure 2.

In the example yod (Figure 2), the yodal configuration is located between the planet Saturn, and the Moon and Sun. The Activating Point is in the ninth house and the Foot is in the third. The Axis of Awareness is from the third house to the ninth, the symbolic yodal pattern. By interpolation, the Sun/Moon midpoint is 12 Scorpio. Saturn is 13 Taurus. Along the Axis of Awareness there will be a midpoint where Saturn and the midpoint energies merge, this is the orb of the Axis of Awareness. This calculates to 12 Taurus/Scorpio

30. This results in the midpoint and the Axis of Awareness having an orb of 30 minutes. This yod contains very tight orbs and indicates a very strong esoteric influence.

In this example, the inconjunct aspects were well within the traditional 2 to 3 degree orbs, but as noted earlier, it is possible to extend that orb with a yod, especially if it is seen to be manifesting in the individual's life in some manner.

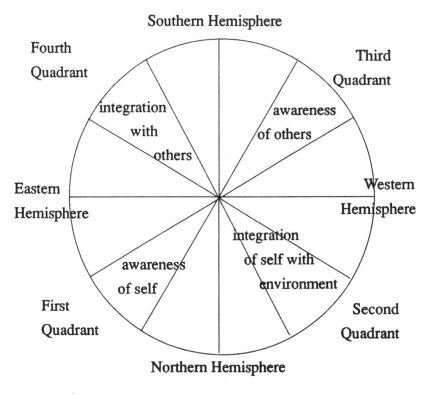

Figure 3.

To begin the synthesis process, determine what hemisphere the yodal points occupy (figure 3). The southern and northern hemispheres are divided by the horizon or first and seventh house axis and the eastern and western hemispheres are divided by the fourth and tenth house meridian. The southern or upper most hemisphere represents the objective nature of the personality and the northern or lower part of the chart represents the subjective and intuitive nature. The eastern hemisphere represents the experiences of the individual that develop a sense of self. The western hemisphere represents experiences that develop a sense of oneself and others.

These hemispheres become the quadrants dividing the chart into four sections. This subject is extensively treated by other authors but a brief review will assist the reader. The first quadrant is between the Ascendant and the fourth house cusp. It represents self-discovery and self-awareness. The second quadrant is between the fourth house cusp and the Descendant. It represents the integration of self with the environment. The third quadrant is between the seventh house and the Midheaven. It represents the awareness of others through relationships. The fourth quadrant is between the midheaven and the Ascendant. It represents the integration of self with others within a social, spiritual and indeed a karmic context.

The use of hemispheres and quadrants is helpful in quickly defining what dimensions the yodal emphasis determines. For instance, if the Activating Point is in the third quadrant, there will be an overall need to develop an awareness of others. In this case, the Foot could be subjectively overemphasizing limiting and detrimental perspectives. In other words this portion of the self would be poorly developed. A southern hemisphere Activating Point would emphasize a need to externalize one's energies to learn to express oneself in an open manner. A further integration of this idea would be an example of a fifth house Activating Point. This could indicate an intuitive, subjective individual with an adaptable nature who may be very influential in the lives of others, possibly children. The idea of hemispheric delineation is rather self-explanatory and was presented as a reminder that it is an important, and often forgotten part of the delineation process. This is especially true for the esoteric astrologer. This quick gestalt delineation, using a few key words, can cut through more traditional and mundane chart analysis techniques to discover important yodal patterns.

With yodal influences interpreted in this manner, clear cut inter-pretations may be gleaned. It is important to remember that a yod may diminish some traditional natal indicators and get the traditional astrologer off target missing the more powerful, subtle and often hidden forces of the yod. Clearly, a strong yodal placement can put an inexperienced astrologer on the wrong track with the result that the client is not assisted in any meaningful manner.

For example, if an individual is outgoing and expressive with many southern hemisphere planets, this would normally indicate a good candidate for a public career. But if there is a yod present and the Activating Point happens to be in the northern or subjective hemisphere, then, this individual, although in many other ways outgoing, will only be able to express his or her special energies in a quiet and internal manner. This will be difficult especially because the Foot of the yod is in the southern hemisphere indicating natural extroversion. For this person it may seem almost unnatural to develop these intuitive subjective energies, yet this is his or her yodal challenge. However, once activated, these energies are a key to a special purpose and direction for the individual.

After determining the objective/subjective nature of the individual, identify any gestalt chart patterns that might exist. These patterns were first introduced by Marc Edmund Jones and are an additional assist in chart delineation and analysis. Some of the patterns such as the bowl, bundle or seesaw may appear to have no yodal aspects. However, with angles and other points included, a yodal configuration may appear in an otherwise unlikely situation. Careful investigation of the chart will be necessary to determine this. The more sophisticated applications such as the inclusion of Uranian planets, midpoint stelliums, lunar nodes and asteroids can be workable but will need careful interpretation because these are a bit more subtle than the traditional astrological indicators.

Finally, do not forget the basic planetary delineations such as element and mode, house and sign position. Although recent research has indicated that some of these factors may not be accurate indicators, they are nonetheless very helpful auxiliary fine tuners of the chart.

It is important to remember that the esoteric interpretation of the yod can exist without the mechanical structure of the chart. It is almost an entity unto itself, specifically because it carries within itself an important spiritual message and lesson for the individual. All of the yodal aspects maintain their own integrity without the other astrological trappings such as house systems. The yod in this definition includes all planets, angles and other factors that are included in the configuration. Keeping this in mind during the delineation will help, although separate chapters on house and sign position have been included, it is the sign and rulership factors that should be more seriously considered because they too, have their own esoteric identities.

Because the yod is an esoteric aspect, by its very nature traditional chart delineation may fall short if a yod or yods are present in the chart. A yod indicates special esoteric, spiritual and soul energies latent within an individual. It will not always be easy to find what timing or life experience is necessary to activate the yod. *In other words, because it is a strong esoteric marker, a yod may remain a virtual road block until activated. This is an important concept.*

All of the traditional astrological resources will be excellent in terms of delineation and interpretation, but for the esoteric astrologer, the yod will require a degree of intuition and spiritual receptivity on the part of the astrologer and the individual to guide the individual properly.

For more information about esoteric astrology, several authors may be helpful on this subject. Although there are many masterful authorities I have found that Joan Hodgson and Martin Schulman present this very complex subject in a simple, readable manner, which is especially appreciated by those unfamiliar with esoteric philosophy, interpretation, concepts and principles.

Joan Hodgson has written several excellent books, namely, *Astrology: The Sacred Science, Wisdom in the Stars,* and *Planetary*

Harmonies. Martin Schulman is especially helpful with the karmic influence of sign and house position in his book, *Karmic Astrology: The Nodes and Reincarnation.*

Yet another author, Torkom Saraydarian, has written a superb esoteric book entitled, *The Symphony of the Zodiac.* It simply presents many profound esoteric components such as rays, planetary constellations and meditations. This book may be a bit too complex for some, but is nonetheless a marvelous source of esoteric astrological and philosophical information.

The reader is encouraged to investigate the esoteric interpretation of the yod. Through this investigation, hitherto unknown and often tantalizingly accurate subtleties contained within the chart will surface.

CHAPTER IV

FIRST HOUSE ACTIVATING POINT
- SEVENTH HOUSE FOOT

The first house traditionally represents the physical body, personality and manner of self expression, one's outlook and attitude toward life. Traditionally ruled by Mars its esoteric ruler is Mercury. Mars represents the vital life force, the life energies of the individual, emphasizing its own reality in a very personal physical manner.

When the yodal configuration has a first house Activating Point, it is important for the individual to develop a strong sense of self. The reason for this is that the Foot of the yod in the seventh house indicates that there is a natural inclination of the individual to defer, even to depend upon a partner or friends. This can result in the assimilation of the partner's mannerisms, ideas, values, outlook and perceptions. Often the charismatic charm and strong needs of others overshadows any concerns for the self and the individual feels comfortable sublimating his needs for the others in the relationship. Ultimately, this can lead to dependence and eventual disappointment with the partner.

Past life influences may have been such that the individual has had this pattern in previous incarnations, may have chosen not to be self responsible, or to ignore responsibility to oneself and others resulting in this present life imbalance.

The esoteric Mercury emphasizes a need to develop a healthy sense of discrimination between the real and unnecessary needs of others. This will help eliminate the potential for overload that is the hallmark of this yodal position. It is important for the individual with this placement to learn to say "No," with no apologies.

With the first house Activating Point, there is a strong need and ability to develop one's own potential and gifts. This is the position of a natural leader, not second in command. This individual always seems to team up with someone who looks as though he is more capable, and certainly wants everyone else to have that impression, but in reality it is his partner with the first house Activating Point that is the power and the brains behind the production. When this is realized, the individual will perhaps begin to utilize his own ideas and insist and this will be a bit tricky - to get credit for himself. This is the whole lesson of the first house Activating Point.

Because of the karmic nature of the yod, all or most of these dynamics will be unknown to the individual. This individual is so easily caught up in the seductive and exciting activities of the other people in his or her life, it never occurs to his or her that he or she should be developing himself or herself. With this aspect, the individual thinks that he needs a partner in his life, but until he has developed his first house appropriately, his partners will only slow him down and block his needed progress. In essence he is asking the partner to provide for him what he needs to develop within himself.

This is a very subtle influence and one of the most difficult because it deals with our personal selves and our understanding of

Errata
The Yod by Joan Kellogg

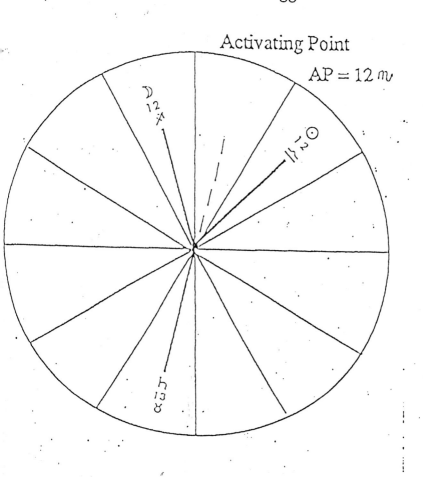

Activating Point

AP = 12 ♏

c one degree orb of the axis of awareness is between 11 Taurus/Scorpio 30 and
Taurus/Scorpio 30, not 12 Taurus/Scorpio 30 as printed.

the relationships that we have with others. This distinction is the most important of all yodal energies because we must have a keen sense of self awareness to be spiritually aware and able to grow. The second difficult dynamic is that it will always involve the complicating presence of other people in our lives and in some ways have much more psychic and emotional pain connected to them. This is the classic co-dependent position and should be of special note to the counseling astrologer.

CHAPTER V

SECOND HOUSE ACTIVATING POINT

- EIGHTH HOUSE FOOT

The second house rules possessions, money, earning power, talents and resources. It is what one values or perceives as valuable. Esoterically, it can be interpreted as one's values and value system however, and to what extent it is developed. One's possessions can also be the skills and talents that one bring with him karmically to be further developed and utilized - sort of a personal contribution - your own tool kit, as it were. It is also where one's personal style of craftsmanship and artistry of life is felt, however it is applied, either by hand, mind or heart. Mundanely it is ruled by Venus which can give Taurus, it's sign, a lovely presence and gentle soul quality. Esoterically it is ruled by Vulcan, the cosmic timekeeper and task-master.

A second house Activating Point indicates that an individual needs to develop an appreciation of his or her own skills and talents. Often self-deprecating, this individual needs to develop a sense of self-worth and to value his or her own abilities. With an eighth-house Foot, this individual's natural inclination is to value the work and talents of others more than his own. His own talents go undeveloped in this aspect because the talents and skills of others are considered more important.

A second/eighth house Axis of Awareness indicates a need to find and develop a healthy and stable place in the world, as defined by the individual, not others. Others are sought as models for this individual's values and ideas of values and talents. This can be the groupie who feels valuable because the group defines his worth, but ultimately has no inner sense of purpose or developed skills to change this perception. This aspect, in its negative connotation, can be one of allowing society in a larger sense to dictate values instead of having them developed from an inner sense of personal compatibility.

The development of one's values occurs early in the individual's life. The importance of the stability and influence of the early caretakers is vital to a healthy, well developed and stable sense of values. Quite often an individual with a second house Activating Point grows up in an environment where there are very strong older role models. The quality of these role models will have a long term effect on the child's world view, especially his or her value system, so it is vital that a positive sense of self be developed from this value system. If the child does not develop a sense of self-worth, it will continue into adulthood resulting in an individual who has no real sense of personal values. His values will always reflect the values of those with whom he has been raised or with whom he is presently with. This can be the sign of the chameleon, the changeable and indecisive personality whose values are not derived from a personal core but from a collective pool.

Vulcan, the esoteric ruler of Taurus, plays an important part in the development of values. Vulcan mythologically was the blacksmith. Wielding his cosmic hammer, he builds and shapes our soul, testing our mettle, continually reshaping us to become finer beings. People with a second house Activating Point will have a crisis of values at some point in their life. This crisis will develop over a critical issue, one in which they are forced to challenge another's, perhaps easier, more popular or even imposed value. The strength to challenge comes when it is sensed intuitively inside that not to challenge the other value, regardless of the cost, would be unconscionable. This will be a real conflict of the soul, a gut-wrenching ordeal. But out of the rubble should be felt the emergence of a personal sense of values born from inner fear and risk, and also from personal morality and ethics. This is the story of the meek and mild mannered person who suddenly stands up to a bully and thereby turns the tide.

This is a difficult position for the Activating Point, but it offers a deep and lasting reward for those willing to grasp and learn its lesson.

CHAPTER VI

THIRD HOUSE ACTIVATING POINT

- NINTH HOUSE FOOT

This is one of the easier yodal configurations to analyze because it represents the symbolic yodal conflict of the development of the third and ninth house Axis of Awareness.

Ruled by Mercury mundanely, the third house represents communication in any form, daily interactions, our early relationships especially siblings and the concept of discrimination and discernment in ideas, thoughts and perceptions. Esoterically, Gemini, ruler of the third house, is ruled by Venus indicating that thought, rightly and correctly motivated, results in communication and action that is guided by love and wisdom, the spiritual ideal.

An individual with a third house Activating Point has a strong philosophical nature. The Foot of the yod is in the ninth house indicating an abundance of lofty ideals, philosophical and abstract concepts, probably an ability to achieve academic success, and perhaps a bit of a disconnection from everyday reality. The third house is underdeveloped indicating the likelihood that this individual has difficulty with practical matters. Even communication may be so rarified that the average person would find it difficult to relate to this individual. Frankly, it is much easier for the Foot of the yod to go off than to face them. But it is just the presence of the third house Activating Point that indicates that in some way some very practical matters need to be addressed or developed in order for this individual to function in a balanced manner. This is the absentminded professor type who can design parking meters but forgets to put the nickels in them.

The third house Activating Point indicates a need to develop the awareness that it is in our small, daily interchanges and interactions with the earth and with one another that we build our happiness and transmute our karma. It is not with the self-designed segregated life lived in philosophical platitudes that anything is accomplished. For some this activity is appropriate and karmically earned and perhaps even necessary, but those with the third house Activating Point have the tendency to ignore the undeveloped mental nature within themselves. They must learn to pay attention to the details of living in order to make their philosophical yearnings and talents more valuable for the rest of us.

When the mental energies of the third house are rebalanced and the individual has submitted to the pedantic and methodological training required for this position, he or she will find that his or her marvelous ninth house capacities, too, improve and the Axis of Awareness becomes alive with practical, usable ideas moderated by idealistic and altruistic motives - a powerful combination.

The third house Activating Point really reflects the untrained mind. It is rather untidy, and must consent to a regular regime of discipline. This is difficult because the ninth house Foot indicates a talented and expansive mind that cannot understand the need for close scrutiny and the careful development of an idea based on a firm foundation. This is the principle behind statistical analysis. It forces the individual with a theory to submit that idea to a practical and methodological manner of testing. If it is valuable, it will withstand the test, if not, it is discounted. The difficulty with the ninth house Foot is that so much of what develops from the mind in not very practical or applicable, it is really intellectual gymnastics at best.

When the third house Activating Point and the Axis of Awareness are developed, a mental and intellectual balance results and we may then find someone who is then able to translate lofty ideas into practical reality. Then the absentminded professor can become the practical inventor, applying some of those marvelous ideas and manifesting them for our service. This is the true mission for the third house Activating Point.

CHAPTER VII

FOURTH HOUSE ACTIVATING POINT
- TENTH HOUSE FOOT

The fourth house traditionally represents the home, the sense and experience of nurturing, usually represented by the mother or parental influence, family values, heritage and ethnic life style. The fourth house also represents one's roots, sense of security and stability or instability. The Moon mundanely rules the fourth house, representing symbolically the past, our karmic ties between our parents and family members, and old patterns of attachment that we experienced in this environment. Esoterically, Cancer, the ruler of the fourth house, is influenced by Neptune. A very subtle and difficult energy to define, it does represent a sense of merging with the nurturing collective unconscious. It represents the maternal archetype, but this ideal is difficult to realize until the earthly lessons of the Moon and Saturn are integrated within the personality.

For a sense of well-being, it is important to have a feeling of security and stability in one's life. This is particularly important in childhood. The fourth house represents the potential building blocks of future relationships. The quality of these relationships will directly reflect the stable or unstable character of the family life that was experienced and that the adult will later build for himself.

The individual with the fourth/tenth house Axis of Awareness has a need to develop a balance between his or her private and public life. A fourth house Activating Point indicates that the individual will emphasize the outer, public world and de-emphasize or even neglect the importance of the inner, private and family world. This may result in the workaholic who sacrifices home life for career and position, perhaps sensing that the public life, even though ultimately quite insecure, nonetheless holds the excitement and stability that the quiet and perhaps unfulfilled private life does not.

An Axis of Awareness between the fourth and tenth house with a fourth house Activating Point represents a weakness of the fourth house energies that need to be developed even though the more attractive tenth house energies seem to lure the individual to more exciting and seemingly more productive work. The fourth house Activating Point indicates that the individual needs to re-evaluate his relationship with himself and his internal roots. This can indicate a person who does not understand the concept or lacks the experience and the sense of internal nurturing, who instead unconsciously seeks nurturing or acceptance through public activity and acclaim.

Tenth house acceptance can be ephemeral, especially if it is built on a poorly laid fourth house foundation. It can be disappointingly transitory and unreliable causing even more turmoil for the individual. True security comes from within and from our efforts to develop a strong inner core, whether from within ourselves or our family. This will be particularly difficult if the Moon, natural ruler of the chart, is the calculated ruler of the fourth house and is afflicted or a part of the yodal configuration. This would typically indicate a poor maternal model or some type of emotional trauma that is the root of the fourth house dilemma.

The lesson of the fourth house Activating Point, then, is to develop a firm sense of one's own roots and internal stability. This may involve the restructuring and abandonment of old, inappropriate family values. More than likely this will be a grief-filled experience, but a necessary one for the next step. Then, when this individual works through the outer, transitory and ephemeral society, he will not be disappointed or disillusioned.

CHAPTER VIII

FIFTH HOUSE ACTIVATING POINT
- ELEVENTH HOUSE FOOT

The fifth house represents creativity of all sorts including procreation, our own unique human creation, our children, and our own inner creative child. It also represents love affairs, pleasures, amusements, speculation, one's avocation, and the manner in which we express our creativity. A strong indicator of artistic or literary talents, especially those connected with such things as are designed for or about children such as children's books or music, this house often indicates the professional who works with children in some capacity. It is mundanely and esoterically ruled by the Sun and Leo. Leo is the sign of the personality, our unfinished selves.

A fifth house Activating Point indicates that the individual lacks an inner discipline or development of the creative portions of his life. With an eleventh house Foot, the individual may be so wrapped up in the creative endeavors of others that his own skills are ignored. This creativity is contributed to the group or organization's efforts to the detriment of the individual's personal talents. These individuals are frequently drawn to organizational or volunteer work, feeling that within the organization there will be a place for them. Ultimately they find that it is their own needs that are stifled in favor of the group's. This is not a bad idea, generally speaking; it is the essence of what is called universal consciousness or brotherhood; but in the case of this yodal configuration, it indicates the individual whose talents must be developed separately. In fact, unless developed independently this individual's talents will not have the opportunity for providing soul growth or real contribution.

Their real contribution lies in the development of their dormant and latent fifth house talents or skills. This can be done within a group context if they are allowed to pursue their own interests. If not, then the fifth house/eleventh house Axis of Awareness can indicate a continual conflict of interests manifesting in power struggles between themselves and others. These individuals will want others to recognize their talents, but in reality, they must validate these talents themselves. This is a very interesting dynamic because in some sense it represents the universal problem of personal skill and talent development. However, the individual with a fifth house Activating Point may be very talented and have multiple potentials, but when asked what it is that he wants to do, may respond that he honestly does not know.

The most serious roadblock to personal development will be the eleventh house Foot. The planet there will indicate the nature of the karmic work to be done to eliminate the blockage. This blockage may be experienced for many years during the individual's life and will be felt as a deep frustration. The planet at the Foot is the key to de-energizing it's restrictive power.

For example, if Saturn is at the Foot of a fifth/eleventh house yodal configuration, then the issue is to deal with authority in a constructive manner. Unfortunately, this can indicate that authority is experienced in an ambiguous and arbitrary manner causing, even intentionally restricting, the individual's life energies. In this case, the fifth house Activating Point must make a break from the system whenever comfortable because ultimately, although the Saturn position also looks as if it insures safety and security, it really only offers restriction. In the early years this may be a necessary discipline applied to an as yet untrained soul; but once the dues are paid, a big Saturn lesson, the fifth house Activating Point can be ready to fly.

Writers, composers and artists of all types are often caught in this squeeze between their need for an eleventh house business income and their true creative fifth house inspirational natures. This is the classic dilemma of creating for others because it pays the bills or for oneself because it satisfies the soul. Adulteration of inspiration can be lucrative, but done too often results in a poverty of the spirit.

A fifth house Activating Point, then, requires that these individuals become aware and acknowledge their special gift of inspiration or talent. Next they need to develop this gift according to their own principles and creativity. Since these people are conduits of divine inspiration, their ideas will then be translated into a universal benefit, not a select one.

CHAPTER IX

SIXTH HOUSE ACTIVATING POINT
- TWELFTH HOUSE FOOT

The sixth house rules matters of health, employment, daily routine and one's sense of service to others. Ruled by Virgo and Mercury mundanely, it is the placement of perfection, a difficult earthly expectation which often manifests as criticism of oneself and others. Esoterically, Virgo is ruled by the Moon, said to be veiling Vulcan. What this means is that the Moon reflects past karmic debts and present opportunities for lessons through service while Vulcan, with its precision hammer, will guide the soul's progress within a very narrow range of opportunities. This is why the Virgo nature appears to have such a limited perspective of things. The sixth/twelfth house polarity represents a particularly potent Axis of Awareness.

With a sixth house Activating Point, the individual must develop a less critical nature, one that synthesizes and produces constructive results from corrected conditions. This is a very difficult lesson because the Foot, located in the twelfth house of karmic and fateful conditions as well as the unconscious mind, has a tendency to keep the individual off balance with the deep unconscious feelings of the needs of others. The Piscean need to lose oneself in service to others, martyrdom really, keeps the individual off track. The great world suffering prevents the individual from seeing his small but important part in alleviating that suffering. It is almost as if the sea of humanity is calling but he forgets that there is sickness at home where he is needed first.

These individuals need to develop realistic perspectives and discrimination - a Mercury lesson. But most importantly they need to develop an understanding of what service and suffering are. Not all suffering is necessary and some of it is self-inflicted through laziness, ignorance or karma. But it is also important for the individual to distinguish between the birds with the broken wings and the buzzards. One needs your help, and when healed, gladly flies away. The other is an opportunist and will pick your bones clean. The twelfth house Foot seems to find the buzzards and the sixth house Activating Point needs to tell them to go elsewhere.

The Axis of Awareness between the sixth/twelfth house is very powerful because of the unconscious nature of the energies. It is important to have a strong personal identity before undertaking work in the larger world. With a twelfth house Foot, it is very easy to quite literally pick up the unconscious vibrations and emanations of the larger whole. If the whole around the individual is sick, sickness can quickly develop. Any and all emotions will be made the individual's and he will quite innocently assume that they are his own. With this axis he must separate the mass thought forms from his own life's direction.

The twelfth house Foot feels the compelling needs of the masses and finds it quite difficult to ignore this suffering and need. The Piscean quality of the twelfth makes it possible to quite literally merge with the collective suffering. Their job with the sixth house Activat-

41

ing Point is to specify what their particular service is and then develop it, not to get lost in the overwhelming needs of others.

The sixth/twelfth house polarity is commonly seen in the chart of the medical professional. A great need to serve those who suffer is answered in developing a competency to handle the crisis. Individuals with a sixth house Activating Point have a need to feel safe and secure within the environment to which they expose themselves. Their twelfth house is so sensitized to everything, including criticism, that it is only in a protected situation that they will venture to their sixth house of service. When this happens their natural and gifted ability to heal is manifested. They can truly be world servers if they so choose, but they must tear down their own walls of illusion to do so effectively.

Within all people with a sixth/twelfth house Axis of Awareness, there is a core of celestial resonance, a natural spiritual harmony. As with all Virgo-related perspectives, if any sense of disharmony is in their presence, they become intolerant and critical, because they know implicitly what the potential for perfection is and should be. This gets in the way, even of their healing powers which are formidable. But because there is so much natural disequilibrium and imbalance in the universe, most people with this placement will need some type of professional assistance or a very stable early environment to help them manage their intense sensitivity, fears and past karmic memories.

Individuals with the sixth house Activating Point need to define their own karma and then differentiate it from the karma of others.

They do not need to take on another's karma to accomplish this goal although they often do and are unable to make this important distinction. Their own karma is sufficient. They must discriminate between their own karma and that of others, indeed the world's, to find their proper and rightful place within the natural order of life.

CHAPTER X

SEVENTH HOUSE ACTIVATING POINT

- FIRST HOUSE FOOT

The seventh house rules the relationships that we have with others. It indicates how we view relationships, what role we designate to ourself and to others within the relationship and what parameters and expectations we have of ourselves and others within that relationship. Mundanely, Venus rules the seventh house, representing the ideal of beauty, love and harmony. Esoterically, Uranus rules the seventh, representing a much finer vibratory influence in the relationship, reflecting the Aquarian ideal of a nonpossessive, nurturing and unconditional love within a relationship. Uranus has no passion of a carnal nature, but rather a passion of the awakened heart that revels in the joy of another spirit's freedom and growth. A marriage of truly enlightened souls and hearts is vastly different than one of jealous, possessive minds. Esoterically, Uranus is all inclusive, mundanely, Venus can be exclusive and separating when expressed in a negative connotation.

Individuals with the seventh house Activating Point have a definite need to develop a sense of the other person within the relationship. With a first house Foot, these individuals are likely to experience relationships from a personal perspective not a shared and mutual one. They quite literally can not imagine that their partner may have personal thoughts, needs and perspectives aside from their own. It is not that they do not think that it is possible, they just rarely develop the awareness that a relationship consists of two people and that the other half coexists with them.

This individual is often introverted, insecure, overly sensitive or self-centered and goes through life isolated from others feelings and an active emotional participation in his or her life. There may be strong tendencies to avoid people, sensing that his presence is counterproductive or harmful. This may be true, certainly in the early years because it has been my experience that individuals with the seventh/first house Axis of Awareness have difficulty discerning the character of others. Their sensitivity and frankness can be too honest and threatening for many so they decide to avoid confrontation. They need to discriminate between hostile and friendly forces.

This individual may feel perfectly content to live within his own self-defined realm. The key to understanding this Axis of Awareness is that the individual's growth is impeded by a continuation of his closed self-centered perspective and that growth only begins when he includes others in his life.

This may present a problem for the seventh house Activating Point because he may well have experienced life with others as unpleasant. He has become distrusting of others and seeks refuge in his own company. With a strong Saturnian aspect to Venus, this will be especially evident in the personality.

Service through cooperative relationships and projects will bring great joy and a sense of reward to this type of individual. There will most likely be a need for the individual to develop better interpersonal communication and relating skills which may and should probably include assertiveness training. This is particularly important because his Venus nature is too sensitive and incapable of defending himself against early harsh experiences and conditioning. The seventh house Activating Point indicates that the individual needs to develop an awareness that doing some things alone is much too hard and difficult not to mention impractical. He frequently finds himself unnecessarily overloaded and overburdened because doing things by himself means that he does not have to deal with anyone else.

The skillful and necessary art of group cooperation and synthesis will allow these individuals to develop their unique talents that go undeveloped because they become too bogged down with inappropriate and unnecessary details that, frankly, another, better qualified individual could manage. The first house Foot indicates that these individuals want to do everything by themselves. A very inefficient way to operate, but it makes perfect sense until it is realized that group work is synergistic. More is achieved as a group than any one of the component parts could achieve by themselves.

When this concept is understood and integrated, the Uranian influence will have begun to manifest in the individual's life and much progress is realized along the spiritual path.

The seventh house Activating Point needs to learn and practice the concepts of cooperation and harmony in relationships.

CHAPTER XI

EIGHTH HOUSE ACTIVATING POINT

- SECOND HOUSE FOOT

The eighth house represents the financial resources of others, others values or valuables, financial obligations such as taxes, and the sexual energy, kundalini, which is the transforming door to higher consciousness. Traditionally, it rules death but this is metaphysically translated as transformation in any form as well as the agents of transformation. The eighth house is co-ruled transforming mundanely by Pluto and Mars. Esoterically, Mars is its ruler. Mars represents the vital life force, the force of the soul to withstand the physical tests of strength required for deep growth. Pluto represents the powerful force that is required for transformation. It is the force of destruction so necessary when old and inappropriate forms must be changed.

In a relationship we are given the opportunity to merge ourselves with another's being on physical, emotional, mental and spiritual levels. The eighth house represents the transforming energies of this other person's presence in our life. How we esoterically merge our values and physically merge our possessions of any nature is an eighth house effect.

Most of us experience the presence of a deep love relationship with another as transforming some aspect of manner of our lives. This may include a sexual aspect or it may reflect a merging of ideals, values and talents with the sexual potential being transmuted from the lower, physical state to a higher, finer vibratory state. If the relationship is deeply bonded, karmic in nature, Pluto, the planet of transformation, will be present as both individuals strive to maintain their individual balance while developing a mutual equilibrium, a new and shared field of energy.

The eighth house Activating Point has a dual effect in an individual's life. First it represents a difficulty for the individual to appreciate or fully understand other perspectives and values. This can also mean universal, spiritual values. An individual with a second house Foot may only understand his own values, perspectives and talents. This may reflect his own internal lack of confidence and value. One can not truly value another until one feels valuable himself. This the individual with the second house Foot must do. If this lesson is not integrated, then this position can indicate a materialistic, selfish and possessive person. This is a very difficult dynamic to encounter in a relationship. The individual may be distrusting, making relationships adversarial. Money, his usual bargaining chip, is symbolic of his inner nature which indicates that he is still stuck to the material world. That is his security. Cooperation and sharing can be an alien concept for the second house Foot, but it is nonetheless an important lesson that must be developed through the eighth house Activating Point.

Secondly, it is the need to understand universal influences in our lives; the idea that there is another force that is constructively building our lives and the idea that nature is a universal cooperative energy that exists, bringing harmony and balance to all living things. The eighth house emphasizes the results of a cooperative or uncooperative attitude about seventh house relationships. If relationships are viewed as a shared and cooperative experience, then an eighth house Activating Point will develop this attribute. But if the second house Foot's influence is evidencing insecurity in the chart, then miserliness in portions of the life may be present with material blockages the result. The roadblocks they give others will be given to them until this stops. This is a particularly difficult lesson because an individual with a second house Foot has often experienced real or feigned deprivation and will feel cheated by the slightest irregularity, demanding due payment from others. He again uses the lowest common denominator of the second house, money, as his medium of communication. Pluto or Mars adversely aspected or in the yodal configuration will aggravate this tendency.

The eighth house Activating Point indicates a need for the individual to develop a respect for another's values and possessions, however, this is interpreted. This may be difficult, especially if early experiences were not very supportive, encouraging or cooperative. When the Activating Point is stimulated, releasing the second house Foot, the Axis of Awareness will begin to bridge this separation and the individual will actually have many more resources available to him than he did before the release. Professionally, this is an indication of the true fiduciary, someone who can be trusted to use his ability to accumulate wealth to be responsible for the nurturing of

49

other's values and possessions. One will then have no feelings of being personally slighted and truly feel honored to be of service to others in a manner consistent with one's interests and talents.

This is the position of the Charles Dickens character, Scrooge, who undergoes a major personality transformation. The differences are remarkable between the old and the new Scrooge. The old Scrooge represented the worst possible second house Foot tendencies and the reformed Scrooge the best of the eighth house Activating Point energies. It is interesting to note that in the story of Scrooge that it was the agent of death, the Plutonian energy, that was responsible for the transformation in his life. The suppressed and sublimated compassion of Scrooge is within all of those individuals with a second house Foot. It just needs to be brought out. But the drama of the story must not be lost because those with a second house Foot can be deeply mired in materiality and may need the eighth/second house Axis of Awareness to be dramatically shaken to cultivate their inner selves. They will most likely need to experience a Plutonian event to release the strangle hold of materiality.

The goal of the eighth house Activating Point, then, is to develop a sense of shared values and universal welfare. Through the experience of deep soul suffering and searching, the second house Foot will release the beautiful inner light and allow it to guide the lives of others who are less fortunate.

CHAPTER XII

NINTH HOUSE ACTIVATING POINT

- THIRD HOUSE FOOT

The ninth house represents the higher mind, that which is capable of spiritual and universal thought. This can be expressed in traditional religious settings, universities, or individual tutorials. The ninth house is traditionally ruled by Jupiter, the expansive principle expressed in a love of travel, physical, astral or otherwise, to experience the ideas and perspectives of many different cultures. Esoterically, Sagittarius is ruled by the Earth, a fitting rulership because it is a misunderstood maxim of the material world that knowledge and insight are gained through outward movement and pursuit. In actuality, it is the development of our higher mind, our soul, experiencing the quiet discipline of an earthly incarnation, the willingness of a soul to be materially confined in a physical body, that offers the most meaningful opportunity for spiritual growth.

This is a difficult placement for the Axis of Awareness because it represents the ninth/third house symbolism of the yod. A third house Foot can indicate a person who is closed-minded, prejudicial and opinionated. These individuals must be left to make their own decisions and opinions about matters. They work best alone, utilizing their unique, if not backward, procedures. The presence of a learning disability can be one of the characteristics of this axis. These individuals do not easily cooperate in the exchange of ideas so essential to the Jupiterian principle of intellectual and emotional expansion required for spiritual growth. If Jupiter in the chart is retrograde this may exaggerate the negative tendencies of the individual. These people can be almost xenophobic, exhibiting a fearfulness of foreign or unfamiliar ideas, people and places.

With a ninth house Activating Point an inclusive attitude will need to be developed. A formalized education will enhance this individual's opportunity for growth as will the opportunity for extensive travel. Parents must insure that a child with this axis has access to a fine educational system. This is their essential foundation. Travel would be best arranged by a tour professional who will make certain that the individual will see all of the valuable sights, not just those that appeal to the close-minded third house Foot. Expansion will only come when exposed to unfamiliar experiences and ideas, not a repetition of that which feels safe and nonthreatening.

Interestingly enough, the ninth/third house Axis of Awareness can be one of the more difficult placements because, although mental fluidity and adaptability are prerequisites for spiritual growth, it is a difficult thing, indeed, to achieve when the mind can not, will not or is not capable of doing so. The third house foot wants to remain stuck in old and familiar nonproductive thought and habit patterns. This axis may also indicate the need for professional help to assist in the training or redirecting of one's learning skills. Quite literally, with a ninth/third house Axis of Awareness, intellectual awareness is the goal and there is no stronger indicator of this than strong planets at the third house Foot. A badly aspected Mercury, ruler of the third, will aggravate this difficulty.

One of the difficulties experienced with this placement is that these individuals may aspire to higher education, but frankly may not have had a supportive foundation to prepare for later academic success. This reinforces their original bias but does not really address the problem of inadequate or improper preparation. Early recognition and treatment of any learning disabilities or reading deficiencies will be a critical factor in later success. Early failures will reinforce already held beliefs of unfairness and strengthen the need to defend oneself through rigid opinions and perspectives.

The ninth house activating Point indicates a need to regard people, their ideas, cultures, philosophies and religions as a part of the harmonic whole, each one symbolizing the expression of a universal principle. Prejudice closes the heart and soul off from the possibility of growth as well as preventing the individual with the ninth/third house Axis of Awareness from learning about his own shortcomings, the road block to growth. These individuals have a strong tendency to project onto others their own inadequacies, thereby gaining a temporary sense of comfort. Those individuals with the third house Foot need to develop a sense, definition and perspective of their own ideas, cultures and perceptions. Once feeling confident and able in their own self-knowledge and experience, they will be free to respect the ideas, experiences and cultures of others.

Respect is one of the biggest lessons for the ninth/third house Axis of Awareness. The earth has many difference types of men and women as represented by different races, cultures, religious creeds and sects. The individual with the third house Foot is here to learn something about the harmonic diversity within the whole. They can be separatists who feel the bitter pain of their own self-imposed separation. They do not understand that to the extent that they are prejudiced, to the same extent they are cutting themselves off from their own natural Jupiterian flow of energy which lies in the ninth house Activating Point. When the ninth house is activated, this individual can become a powerful force for unification through universal educational and philosophical principles. This can be accomplished through publishing, travel and teaching in what ever manner or mode.

The lesson of the ninth house Activating Point, then, is that a larger world perspective must be sought through the development of a stable understanding of and a sound respect for the ideas of others.

CHAPTER XIII

TENTH HOUSE ACTIVATING POINT

- FOURTH HOUSE FOOT

The tenth house rules the outer world and the way we present ourselves to the world as participants in mutual responsibility. It is here that we are identified by the talents, interests and abilities that we express in our career and professional lives. Our choice of work indicates how we most comfortably express our unique and individual energies. Parental influences can be very important here as the tenth house represents that parent who served as the teacher and representative of the social structure. In a yodal configuration, parental influences are integral to understanding the individual's career choices, goals and motivations, all important components of their sense of mission.

Saturn rules the tenth house mundanely and esoterically, doubly emphasizing the importance of an individual's responsibility within the world community. It also emphasizes the responsibility of each individual to find and discharge his or her own duties and responsibilities within the world around him or her. The fourth house represents the early years, family life, structure and responsibility, learned concepts of mutual aid and support.

The tenth house represents our mature responsibility to contribute our talents and take responsibility for the larger world. This can be done by actively taking a role in governmental and political affairs at whatever level one is attracted. This also means choosing a service that will be productive for ourselves and our society. We refer to this as our job, career or profession. We carry the lessons of the fourth house into our tenth house experiences.

The tenth house Activating Point indicates an individual who has some special talent to offer the larger community but because of some misconception is confined to a limited role of duty and obligation, usually with strong family overtones. This perception may be limited to one's family or close circle or perhaps within one's religious, ethnic or racial grouping. Responsibility is the key word with this Axis of Awareness and the individual will need to grow away from the confines of limited family security and responsibilities to a larger and more global perspective of responsibility. This is a difficult dynamic because of the clannish nature of the Cancer-ruled fourth house Foot. This role may be inappropriately thrust upon the individual by the family or group. This position also indicates where the lesson of individual and group responsibility must be learned before larger responsibility can honestly and freely be undertaken.

Often the individual with the tenth house Activating Point seeks family security instead of growing toward accepting group responsibility. The neglect of the group responsibility is a weak point in the individual. The individual needs to discern what responsibility is and just what his individual role within the smaller and larger units may be. This apparent neglect and desire to abandon group responsibility for family security will be the single most important lesson for the individual to learn. The larger, seemingly unimportant responsibilities must be learned and valued in preparation for more important duties. Lasting public success and respect will evade these individuals until they have learned to accept responsibility for their larger role. This can be the citizen who refuses to carry out civic responsibility such as voting or participating in important civic duties when he may be called upon or in a position to assist. The ability to make sound value judgments in this area is critical and will be a strategic tool for the individual when learned.

Individuals with a fourth house Foot will seek worldly recognition prematurely or shun it in favor of either neglecting or becoming immersed in family exclusivity. They seek the comfort of the family forgetting that all larger groups only represent the individual who symbolizes all of our needs. If we have slighted the group to gain the glory of the individual we have not learned our lesson.

The fourth house represents the early structure that was provided and built for us through our family. The tenth represents the structure that we must build for ourselves, our own home in the world as it were. Our interests and perspectives of the world more or less determine the structure that is built around us, the types of business associates with whom we are likely to deal, the interests that we share with others, and the nature of our work. Incomplete and unsatisfactory fourth house lessons will hinder our progress towards building this important life structure.

A tenth house Activating Point indicates that through the individual's contact with the outer world, regardless in what capacity they may become more fully actualized and spiritually in tune through the lesson of appropriate responsibility. To accomplish this these individuals must cut away old, outworn, inappropriate and shortsighted ideas and attitudes as indicated by the fourth house influence. They need to grow beyond themselves and merge with the collective group as responsible citizens of the world. With a fourth house Foot this is not easy, life as it is in the small, comfortable confines is too attractive, but ultimately disappointing and not where the individual's true service lies.

CHAPTER XIV

ELEVENTH HOUSE ACTIVATING POINT
- FIFTH HOUSE FOOT

The eleventh house traditionally rules hopes, friends, wishes, organizations and income from business. Mundanely, Uranus rules Aquarius, ruler of the eleventh. Esoterically, Jupiter rules the eleventh. Uranus represents the eclectic and electromagnetic nature of man, the individuality within the harmonic whole. Jupiter represents the unifying principle through education and enlightenment. This house represents the ideals of the Aquarian Age - the age of LIGHT in all things. It represents the ability to synthesize our differences within a harmonic vibration.

One's social comfort level develops from the fourth/tenth house axis. If there has been much encouragement in the early home life and the tenth house abilities unblocked than the tenth house potential of group responsibility blends well with the eleventh/fifth house Axis of Awareness. This axis represents the use of creative differences of mankind. The eleventh house represents the peacemaker, the negotiator and diplomat. With an eleventh house Activating Point we find the potential group leader hiding in individual enterprise, the avid reclusive hobbyist and the reticent and reluctant group joiner. Just as we saw the eleventh house Foot reveal a tendency to develop useless and unnecessary group affiliations, in the eleventh house Activating Point we find individuals who have a distaste for organizations, preferring to go about their business by themselves. They are invariably lonely because of this attitude, but they stick to it with a fierce tenacity. It is often the case that their own fifth-house creativity was stifled or underdeveloped and now, in a need to defend what precious sense of integrity they retain, they maintain an underdeveloped potential to their great regret. When they develop a group consciousness, their true talents as mediator and facilitator can be realized. No man is an island, although many with the eleventh house Activating Point find themselves living just such a life. They need to learn interdependence and group productivity, the result of shared talents and skills.

The planets involved in the yod and their rulerships will indicate more detailed clues as to the source of the reluctance to merge with and contribute to organized society.

An individual with an eleventh house Activating Point has to develop interests within a group, to experience life as a mutual participant, not as an observer. This Axis of Awareness indicates a person with marvelous group facilitation and management skill potential but who feels uncomfortable within the confines of a group. The fifth house Foot has a natural reticence to relinquish its coveted privacy, it insures one a criticism-free environment. But it is only through group work that one's true service emerges. This Axis of Awareness truly represents the lesson of the New Age - group service.

As a team member, the individual with the eleventh house Activating Point can be the person who joins disparate factions, genuinely understanding and respecting the different perspectives and uniting them together. This Activating Point position represents the symbolic bridge between separation and unification.

The goal of the eleventh house Activating Point is to develop a sense of group participation knowing that it is through the group, not through solitary efforts, that their true service emerges.

CHAPTER XV

TWELFTH HOUSE ACTIVATING POINT
- SIXTH HOUSE FOOT

The twelfth house mundanely represents the unconscious mind, karma, restriction including imprisonment, large institutions, personal weakness relating to karmic lessons and the collective unconscious. Mundanely, the twelfth, ruled by Pisces, is traditionally ruled by Neptune, although some esoteric authors ascribe Jupiter to this position. Esoterically, Pluto rules this sign, again with some authors indicating Jupiter. In either case, the twelfth house is one of deep spiritual significance and mystery and not easily delineated either mundanely or esoterically. The soul stores its secrets there and only the most masterful may gain access to and be trusted with the karmic responsibility of opening the books of the akasha preserved there.

The Virgo-ruled sixth house tends to emphasize the detail at the expense of the greater whole. A sixth house Foot indicates persons who would have a difficult time breaking away from daily, ingrained rigid habit patterns that reinforce their emphasis of the particular. They have difficulty developing a larger karmic pattern. They easily become bogged down in needless minutia which can lead to physical tension and mental exhaustion. Perfectionism, however expressed or perceived, is so strong a personality characteristic that these individuals quite literally become unable to see the forest for the trees.

They struggle to get out of their self-defined muddle, but don't quite see how they are self-defeating, almost from the beginning.

As in all astrological delineation, all aspects must be modified based upon other factors in the chart. However, the twelfth/sixth house Axis of Awareness is a very difficult one and an individual can be at any level of development between the sixth and twelfth house energies; so generalities must be made in order to be safe in the interpretation. Care must be taken to see how these energies are used so as to not upset the ultrasensitive individual with this Axis of Awareness.

Sensitivity is an important part of the twelfth/sixth house Axis of Awareness. In its lower manifestation, the sixth house Foot indicates a high-strung character, susceptible to many and varied illnesses, most of which indicate either an acute sensitivity to environment or a resistance to change. A key to the solution of this condition is to learn the ability to flow with the daily energies of life, not to resist, analyze or criticize. What they resist is what they know to be imperfect, and yet they do not realize that in concentrating on that imperfection they, too, become crystallized and impede progress. They will need to work on their own personality issues to be of ultimate value. This is very frustrating for them.

From professional experience, this can be one of the most in-trenched individuals because they only see the goal not the process, the perfection not the practical or perhaps the real, however, they define it. They may have what is clinically referred to as magical thinking and yet within them they have the key that most of us lack.

We need to listen wisely and then help them out of their self-imposed labyrinth.

Tread carefully with either the sixth or twelfth house yod, they bear similar dynamics in this regard. They are excruciatingly sensitive which only serves to indicate the beauty and love present in the soul. When the twelfth house energies begin to develop the perfection that has been so dearly sought in the incomplete whole, then will the collective energies as represented by the twelfth house cohere for this individual.

The sixth house emphasis seems to indicate individuals who are unable to share responsibilities. They feel as if they must do all of the work themselves. Who better prepared than a perfectionist?

The energies represented by the twelfth house are very confusing for the undeveloped personality. The Piscean element is difficult to negotiate because of its nebulous and apparently indefinable nature. In actuality, the definition becomes clear as one learns to negotiate the unfamiliar spiritual realms and leaves the apparently certain nature of earthly laws. Pisces is symbolic of the forgotten spiritual essence within us and the mystical laws that govern our spiritual lives. For some with this placement it needs to be rediscovered or preserved. Others may need to relearn its meaning.

The twelfth house Activating Point can clearly indicate an individual with a karmic mission and purpose in life, not just a lesson. There will be a great reluctance to leave the security offered by the sixth house, matter-of-fact daily nature, but once the Axis of Awareness is stimulated and movement begins toward the twelfth house, a world leader, an avatar can appear to help heal the planet.

Our collective unconscious is as receptive and in need of healing as is our physical body. It is here in the twelfth house that the dynamic of healing is altered to reflect the higher vibrations of the approaching Aquarian Age. Instead of healing in an individual, separate Virgoan manner, the twelfth house Activating Point represents the ability to be aware of and heal our collective karma. We, as a planet, are in the process of a major healing. This is the essence of the mission of those with the twelfth house Activating Point. Their mission is to develop this inner desire for universal peace and harmony and begin to realize that their abilities lie not in individual consciousness but in world consciousness.

This can be done on several levels. For instance, many are able to heal the planet through constructive group meditation and service efforts. There is no ego benefit in this, just the understanding that this is a necessary and appropriate service. It is an understood obligation as a member of the human race. Few will in actuality reach the status of a saint, indeed, few need to. Much can and is done just having the consciousness and the awareness that there is an essential work to perform, and then performing it.

The esoteric Plutonian energies will insist on no less than a total transformation of mankind to accomplish the goal of planetary healing. A complete transformation of perspective is required and the self-limiting sixth house Foot will transform to the all-encompassing and compassionate twelfth house Piscean perspective.

Individuals with the twelfth house Activating Point will need to eliminate selfish or closed perspectives, denying or ignoring their own need to heal within the larger healing process. When they begin to realize that by participating in the planetary healing, they will heal themselves, they then will gladly give of themselves to others. Theirs is the lesson of selfless service. It may be within traditional social institutions or within nontraditional Aquarian organizations such as holistic health clinics or professional occupations that allow a free-dom of expression. And by giving they receive immeasurable joy and love.

CHAPTER XVI

FINAL THOUGHTS

The previous chapters have delineated the interpretation of the yod throughout the houses. As was mentioned earlier, a bit of interpretive license will give the reader a much fuller and broader application of the yodal theory. For instance, perhaps the yod may be a fifth/eleventh house yod. Natally, the fifth/eleventh house is the Leo/Aquarius axis. When researching the necessary information, it is again advised that the reader check information on the fifth/eleventh as well as the Leo/Aquarius axis. These subtle differences add significant depth to the delineation. The previously mentioned Martin Schulman book is an excellent source for this research.

Another important application which I shall develop in the next book is that of synastry. In chart comparisons I have found that yodal configurations that aspect in some significant manner affect the relationship in some way. For example, one typical case of repression is represented by the Saturn of one partner being at the Foot of another. This is a classic karmic position that might otherwise have been neglected without the utilization of the Activating Point and Foot axis in the chart. Conversely, another example might be the Sun on the Activating Point stimulating a person to develop his or her higher potential. For instance, a therapist's Venus or Jupiter may activate the yod or an employer's Jupiter or a teacher's Saturn conjuncting an Activating Point will greatly benefit and discipline an individual in a meaningful way.

It is important to remember that the yodal energies flow back and forth on the Axis of Awareness so that the real definition of the effect of the placement depends upon the level of personal awareness and maturation of the individual as well as his own personal psychology. This must always be taken into consideration before any chart is analyzed, especially esoterically.

When writing this book the intention was to present the theory and its basic application in a simple and easily readable format. A second book is planned to incorporate more advanced techniques that are workable with a yod. It will also include a question and answer portion for those astrologers who may have experience or information that may help to broaden the information base on this subject. Case histories will be included and all readers are invited to send what information they may have of interest for inclusion in the book.

Please include in your information a copy of the astrological chart, pertinent data about the individual and a history of events or experiences relating to the yodal influence. Be certain to include your name, address and telephone number. All information will be gratefully received and acknowledged.

Please send all information to:

Joan Kellogg
c/o AFA
P. O. Box 22040
Tempe, AZ 85285

APPENDIX

Single Yods

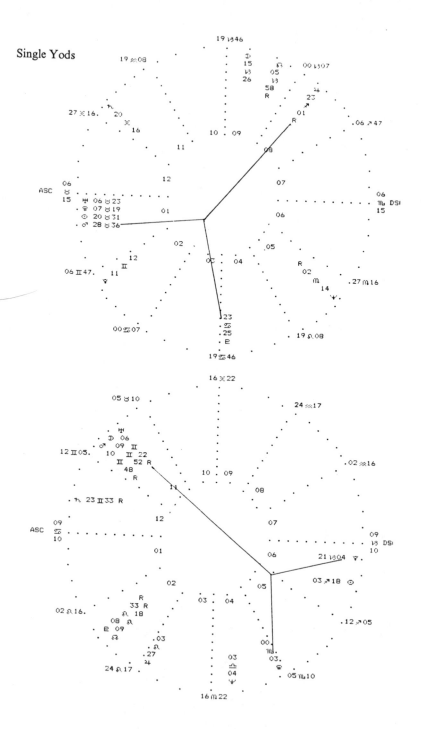

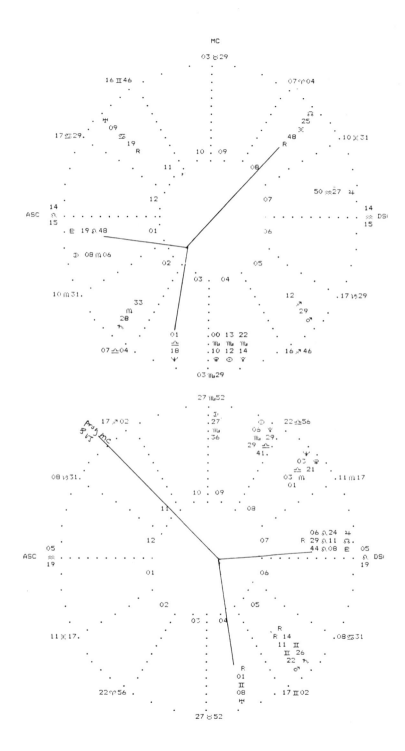

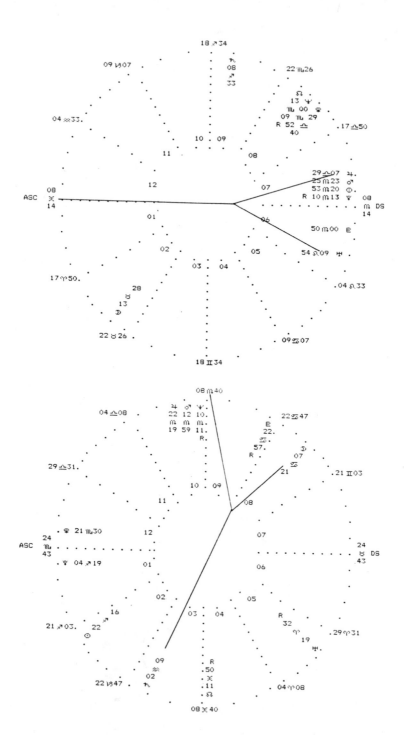

Transiting Yod -- Pluto in Scorpio

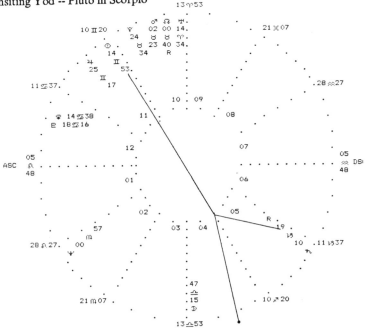

Two Yods

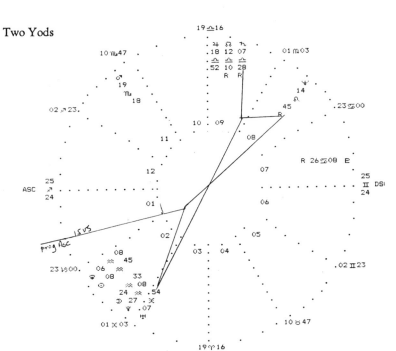

Two Double Yods

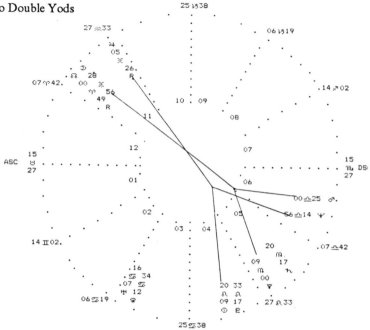

Three Double Yods and Two Single Yods

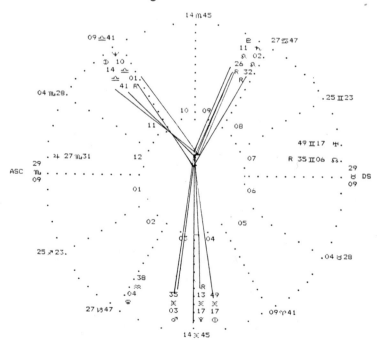

Quadruple Yod

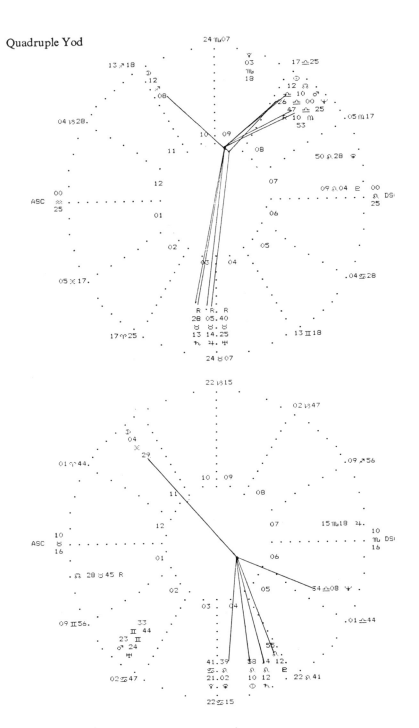

This edition of
The Yod: Its Esoteric Meaning
was word-processed using Sprint,
a product of Borland International,
and reproduced in Postscript mode
using Xerox Ventura Publisher,
a product of Xerox Corporation.

This edition of
The Yod: Its Esoteric Meaning
was word-processed using Sprint,
a product of Borland International,
and reproduced in Postscript mode
using Xerox Ventura Publisher,
a product of Xerox Corporation.